VULTURES

VULTURES

Mark J. Rauzon

A First Book

FRANKLIN WATTS   *A Division of Grolier Publishing*
New York • London • Hong Kong • Sydney • Danbury, Connecticut

For Michael and Raymond—
Fly free forever.

Frontispiece: A flock of white-backed vultures feed.
Photographs ©: Animals Animals: 40, 56 (Henry Ausloos), 50 (John Gerlach),
18, 44 (Gérard Lacz), 30 (Zig Leszczynski), 3 (Stefan Meyers), 33 (Wilf Schurig),
27 (Peter Weimann); Art Resource: 52 (Bildarchiv Foto Marburg); Photo Researchers: 36
(John Borneman), 8, 24 (Nigel Dennis), 38 (Kenneth W. Fink), 47 (M. P. Kahl),
43, 55 (Tom McHugh), 23 (Mark Newman), 29 (Rod Planck), cover (Leonard Lee
Rue III), 20 (M. H. Sharp); Superstock, Inc.: 13, 14; Visuals Unlimited: 11,
58 (John Gerlach), 35 (Milton H. Tierney, Jr.).

Library of Congress Cataloging-in-Publication Data

Rauzon, Mark J.
Vultures / Mark J. Rauzon.
p. cm. — (A First book)
Includes bibliographical references (p.) and index.
Summary: Describes the physical characteristics, behavior,
and different species of these scavenger birds.
ISBN 0-531-20271-2 (lib.bdg.)   ISBN 0-531-15853-5 (pbk.)
1. Vultures—Juvenile literature. [1. Vultures.] I. Title. II. Series.
QL696.F32R38 1997
598.9˙16—DC20   96-31019
                                                        CIP AC

CONTENTS

VULTURES

A bearded vulture soars through the sky on the lookout for animal carcasses.

SCAVENGERS BY NATURE

High in the sky, a vulture soars in lazy circles. From its bird's-eye view, it can see for miles in every direction. On the horizon, it spies a flock of black birds swooping to the ground. The vulture folds its wings to fly a little faster. The wind whistles through its pinion feathers, flared out in flight. The vulture joins a flock circling over a dead cow. The birds land and begin to pick out the eyes of the decaying animal.

When an animal dies, vultures serve as clean-up crew and garbage collectors. By eating the remains of dead animals, they remove smelly, putrid, germ-bearing carcasses called carrion and help prevent the spread of disease. In doing so, vultures perform an important role in the environment.

Recycling leftovers is the vulture's lot in life. These birds are scavengers (animals that live on decayed matter), not predators (animals that kill other animals for food). Vultures recycle protein found in meat, which they need in order to live, grow, and reproduce.

As the undertakers of the bird world, vultures have always been associated with death. With their hunched backs, naked heads, and practice of sticking their heads into rotting bodies to eat decomposing flesh, they may be many people's least favorite animals.

Vultures, however, are beautifully adapted to their calling. For example, if they had feathered heads, they would become soiled with blood and guts. In the hot climates where they live, they would stink and spread diseases harmful to others and themselves. Instead, they have naked heads, which are easier to keep clean.

Another way vultures have adapted to the practice of scavenging is their ability to fly with little effort. Their wide wings make flying easy. Gliding like an airplane instead of flapping their wings saves them a lot of energy and allows them to fly many miles looking for food without getting tired. Because vultures do not know where or when their next meal is, they need to conserve their energy.

Three white-backed vultures pick the bones clean.

Scientists used to think that vultures were related to hawks and eagles because they have several physical features in common. Hawks, eagles, and vultures have hooked beaks and wide wings for soaring flight. And their food preferences are similar, because some eagles and hawks also eat dead animals.

But important differences have always existed between these groups of birds. The vulture's beak is hooked like a hawk's, but it is not as sharp. Vultures sometimes must wait days for a carcass to rot enough for them cut it open with their beaks. Vultures also have weak feet. They lack the claws, or talons, that hawks have for grasping and killing their prey, nor can vultures close their feet in a death grip. Their noise-making also differs. Vultures can only hiss and grunt while hawks and eagles scream.

Other differences between vultures and hawks and eagles abound. During the mating season, vultures dance by jumping up and down, snap their bills, and puff out air sacs in their necks. Hawks do a sky dance that includes midair tumbling and grabbing each other's

Like vultures, hawks have hooked beaks and wide wings.

feet in flight. During the nesting season, mated pairs of vultures share duties. For hawks, only the female usually sits on the eggs. And when the eggs hatch, hawks bring fresh meat, which they tear into bite-sized morsels. Vultures feed their chicks by regurgitating—bringing up partially digested food—from their stomachs into the mouths of their young.

Vultures also have a unique, if disgusting, method to cool off during hot weather. The bird pees on its own legs to lower its body temperature. Because birds do not have separate bowels and bladders, their excrement is watery. They spray it on their feet and legs in a process called urohidrosis. As the liquid evaporates, it cools them off like a personal air conditioner and stains their legs white. When vultures do take a bath, they dip one wing into the water, dunk their head, and spill water over their backs. Hawks dip their breast feathers in and shake their wings to splash water over their backs.

In fact, some vultures act more like storks than like hawks. Storks dance the same way vultures do, have

Storks and vultures share many physical characteristics.

air sacs that they inflate when courting, feed their chicks regurgitated food, and spray excrement on their legs to cool off. The stork's internal bone structure is similar, their feathers and muscles show similar growth patterns, and both types of birds have open nostrils that you can see through.

Ornithologists, scientists who study birds, conducted special tests from blood samples of vultures and storks. In every cell—the body's smallest building block—of our bodies, genes tell the cells how to grow and operate. Genes contain units of DNA, a chemical blueprint of our past. By examining patterns of DNA, scientists can compare various species. Related animals show similar DNA patterns, because the information in the genes is as old as the species itself. Because thousands and thousands of generations change the genes very little, DNA shows how an animal evolved over time and how it is linked to its past.

DNA testing proved that there are two different groups, or families, of vultures. One family evolved on the continents of the North and South America—at one time called the New World—and is known as New World vultures. The other vulture family evolved on the continents of Europe, Africa, and Asia—once called the Old World—and is known as Old World vultures. The seven species of New World vultures are related to storks, but the fifteen species of Old World vultures are related to hawks.

With their long, broad wings, vultures can soar effortlessly on air currents for hours.

ENERGY SAVERS AND RECYCLERS

Old World vultures and New World vultures have featherless heads, excellent eyesight, and long, flat wings to help them survive. These similar features are an example of a biological principle called convergent evolution. Convergent evolution is when unrelated groups of animals separately develop similar physical characteristics.

When the wind conditions are right, vultures can soar for hours and hours, looking for other vultures to make a move and waiting for a sick animal to die. Vultures seek out updrafts of warm air called thermals to carry them high in the sky. Flapping their wings infrequently, they coast on the wind and steer by cocking their tail to one side or another and shifting their

wing positions. They glide with hardly a wing beat and can search over 100 miles (161 km) a day.

When a thermal gives out, vultures glide away and slowly descend until they find another rising thermal, which effortlessly lifts them up like a sky-high elevator. From high altitudes, they can see for miles and miles and, with their keen eyesight, keep an eye on other vultures. And white spots on some vultures' wings help them see each other from afar. If they see others landing, it's a signal that a dead animal has been found and dinner is served!

Sunbathing is another energy-saving behavior of vultures. After a cold night, vultures spread their long wings in the early morning light to help them heat up their bodies, which have cooled down during the night. The dark feathers help absorb heat and regain the bird's normal body temperature. Then, they wait for the sunlight to heat up the ground, which in turn creates thermals of warm air that rise into the sky. Late in the morning, the vultures are ready to leave their perches

Stretching its wings in the sun, a turkey vulture warms up after a cold night.

to ride the thermals into the sky and begin searching for food again.

For vultures, it is a race to find a carcass, even as one as small as a dead mouse, before other scavengers do. Other scavengers include crows, skunks, dogs, opossums, crabs, and catfish. For all these scavengers, a dead animal is a free piece of protein that requires little energy to obtain. In nature, nothing is wasted.

Vultures must get to the carcass soon after the animal dies. They smell the stench of dead meat as they fly low over the treetops. When the smell is ripest, they land on the ground to improve their searching abilities. People used to think that an extremely rotten carcass attracted the most vultures, but experiments have proven that vultures prefer fresh meat over rotten meat. A very hungry vulture, however, will eat meat in almost any stage of decay.

Scavengers must also race against the decomposers. Dead meat starts to smell within twelve hours and quickly decomposes due to bacteria already present in the meat. Bacteria speeds up the decay process by rapidly reproducing and creating poisons, or toxins, to prevent other organisms from eating the meat. They give off the foul odor of decaying flesh. Flies and other

Vultures feast on a rotting zebra carcass.

A group of hungry white-backed vultures
devour the remains of a large elephant.

insects are usually first to find a carcass. Flies lay their eggs and the larvae, or maggots, secrete enzymes into the meat, breaking it down into a liquid that the maggots drink. In hot weather, with help from maggots, bacteria can reduce a corpse to skin and bones in just a few days.

The large, dead animals that vultures seek may be few and far between. So when vultures find a carcass, they must eat as much as they can. The great English naturalist, Charles Darwin, reported that Andean condors, which are large vultures, can go up to six weeks without food. In contrast, hummingbirds expend so much energy that they have to eat every half hour. Vultures may not be able to fly after a heavy meal, so they sit on the ground and digest their food. If predators come by and vultures need to lighten their load, they regurgitate some food until they can get airborne.

NEW WORLD VULTURES

Turkey vultures are the most common members of the New World vultures in North America. They range throughout the United States and into Canada during the summer. Turkey vultures, also known as "TVs" to bird-watchers, do not build nests but lay one to two creamy-white eggs with red-brown dots in rock crevices, abandoned hawk nests, dense underbrush, or caves. In winter they migrate out of the colder regions and fly to Mexico and Central and South America, to the tip of Tierra del Fuego, and also to the islands of Cuba and Jamaica.

Some people call turkey vultures "turkey buzzards." Buzzards are a kind of hawk that lives in Europe. Early colonists in America thought they recognized the birds from England and the name stuck.

A flock of turkey vultures roost together.

Turkey vultures can be easily identified by their gray-and-black wings with long "fingers" pointing out at the wingtip and their rocking manner of flight. Using their wings, which are slightly upcurved—not flat like an eagle's—these vultures teeter and tilt in flight, as the wind carries them across the sky. Recently, several low-flying aircraft have flown into turkey vultures and crashed.

Turkey vultures are one of only a few kinds of birds that can smell. Turkey vultures have a highly developed olfactory organ in their brains, finely tuned to smell the slightest whiff of rotting meat. Their nostrils are open slits on their beaks. As they fly, passing back and forth in the air, they sniff the wind flowing through their nostrils and follow the scents of decay to their source, like a shark honing in on blood.

Turkey vultures are named after wild turkeys because of their small, red heads. Ornithologists have observed that, for some turkey vultures, the red color deepens when they are at a feast. The darker color signals to other turkey vultures that they "rule the roost" and feed before others with pinker heads.

With the exception of their different colored heads, two other groups of New World vultures look very

Turkey vultures have an excellent sense of smell, which helps them locate carrion.

similar to the turkey vulture. The lesser yellow-headed vulture is common near forest edges, wet fields, and open marshlands of South and Central America. The greater yellow-headed vulture is common in undisturbed rain forests well away from human settlements in South America's Amazon River. Like the turkey vulture, it too can smell.

Black vultures have benefited from some of the changes humans have made to the environment. A long time ago, black vultures were restricted to marshes and swamps. As human settlements developed in low-lying areas, the vultures moved into the surrounding woods. In many towns in Central and South America, black vultures are the most common bird, fighting with stray dogs and chickens over table scraps.

Black vultures are the most social of vultures. They flock together at night to sleep, preen each other, and defend against nighttime attacks. Black vultures are unique in that they hunt in family groups; up to twenty-two have been counted on a carcass. At the

The black vulture is the most common vulture in South America.

carcass, vultures squabble over the spoils. They have no voice box so they hiss and grunt, sometimes biting and tugging on each other's feathers.

Because of their short wings, black vultures need strong thermals to help them take off. Once airborne, they form kettles—large flocks of birds circling high in the air—for hours. Black vultures have excellent eyesight. When they see turkey vultures land, they fly in to investigate. On the ground, their large feet are useful for holding down food and running a loping, sideways hustle while they rustle their black feathers. Black vultures forage around towns and highways looking for animals hit by cars, but sometimes they may kill small animals themselves. If they find a big animal, they eat the eyeballs first, and then wait for the larger vultures to appear.

When king vultures arrive to feed, all the other vultures get out of the way. A king vulture will tear into the tough hides of dead cattle with its strong beak, making food available for other vultures. The king vulture eats the meat while black vultures go for the guts and even enter inside the body. Turkey vultures feed slowly on the leftovers that remain on the bones. Together, they can pick a cow carcass clean in a few hours.

The colorful king vulture rules the forest.

The king vulture is white and black with a colorful head. White eyes stare out of its yellow-and-purple face with orange wattles of skin hanging from its nose. They soar very high up in the sky alone or in pairs. Silent in flight, they fly steadily as they wait for turkey vultures to locate food.

Vultures eat as much as they can and store the food in their crop before it goes to the stomach. The crop fills up and sticks out. It is a signal to others at the feast who is at the top of the pecking order. The crop is red in the turkey vulture, pink in the king vulture, and yellow in the condor.

Condors are giant vultures with broad wings that spread over 10 feet (3 m) across! The largest bird in North America is a condor—the California condor. There are two kinds of condors and each has a continent to itself: the Andean condor of South America and the California condor of North America. Both kinds of condors have white patches on their magnificent black wings that help the birds keep track of each other.

Condors live as long as sixty years. Females condors lay one or two white eggs, which are $4\frac{1}{2}$ inches (11 cm) long. They take forty-five to fifty-five days to hatch.

California condors may only breed once every other year. The chick spends five months in a cave or

These courting king vultures have prominent pink crops.

A rare California condor streaks through the air.

hollow tree nest and is fed regurgitated food by both parents. The young are dependent on their parents for nine months after they can fly. During this period, they learn how to find food, water, and nesting sites. The gray-headed immatures take five to seven years to reach adult plumage and begin reproducing. At breeding time, they sway their orange or pink heads and inflate their yellow crop as a sign of readiness to mate.

Over fifteen thousand years ago, during the Pleistocene Ice Age when great mammals like the woolly mammoths and saber-toothed tigers lived, California condors ranged from Canada to Mexico and from the Atlantic coast to the Pacific. Condor fossils have been found in Florida and New York.

In the last five hundred years, the condors' range shrank to the western mountains and the Pacific coast area, where dead whales, seals, and antelope and buffalo herds were available. Flocks of condors migrated to the Columbia River, which flows into the Pacific Ocean, when the salmon were running. As human populations expanded, however, the California condor populations declined further until they became one of the most endangered of all species.

Although Andean condors are not as rare as California condors, they are absent in areas in which

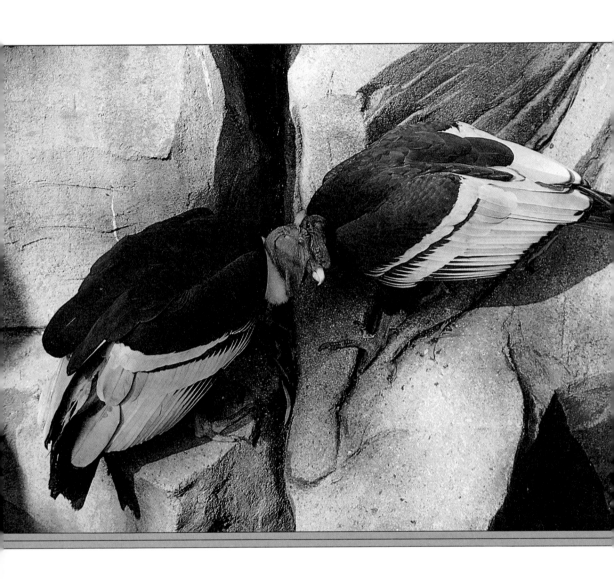

A pair of Andean condors court on a rocky ledge.

they were once common. Andean condors prefer rocky cliffs, steep canyons, and shallow mountain caves, where they can nest and roost undisturbed. They ride the freezing winds of South America's majestic Andes Mountains to the coasts of Peru and Chile. Along the shorelines, Andean condors eat dead whales, sea lions, and seabird eggs. In the mountains, they eat dead live-stock and scour the slopes looking for animals killed in snow avalanches.

Andean condors are the only New World vultures to show sexual dimorphism, which is when the males differ in appearance from the females. Males have a large fleshy crest and neck wattles, which the females lack.

Egyptian vultures live in the warm, dry regions of Europe and Asia.

OLD WORLD VULTURES

DNA evidence proves that Old World vultures are not related to New World vultures. Old World vultures are hawks and eagles in disguise. Generally, so-called Old World vultures live in open areas, grasslands, mountains, and deserts while New World vultures, with the exception of condors, are more forest birds.

One Old World vulture does depend on forests. The unique palm-nut vulture of central Africa is mainly a vegetarian, eating palm nuts that it sometimes gathers by hanging upside down.

Other Old World vultures use special skills to get food. Egyptian vultures are among the handful of animals besides humans that use tools. They have learned to pick up rocks with their long, thin beaks and fling them against the giant eggs of ostriches. The thick eggshell of the ostrich needs several blows from the rocks before it cracks. Two quarts (1.9 l) of yolk will feed a whole flock of vultures. Egyptian vultures are common in Africa, especially around villages where they eat a variety of garbage, excrement, and carrion.

After all the other vultures have fed, the bearded vulture cleans up. Also known as the lammergeier, the bearded vulture has stiff bristles under its beak, bright yellow eyes, and a feathered head, for this bird does not get into blood and guts.

Bones make up most of the bearded vulture's diet. The vulture is after the marrow inside the bone, where the body makes blood. Bearded vultures will swallow small bones whole, but big bones are more troublesome. In the same way that gulls drop clamshells on the boardwalk to get to the food inside, bearded vultures drop bones on a flat rock called an ossuary to crack the bones open. The birds pick up bones and fly high into the air, dropping them again and again until they are broken enough to be eaten. The bearded vulture's stomach acid is so strong, it digests all of the bones. Large bones are sometimes stored at nest caves to smash later.

Old World vultures, like this bearded vulture,
have stronger beaks than New World vultures.

The griffon vulture is named after a mythical beast having the body of a lion and the wings and head of an eagle.

Griffon vultures are the largest and highest-flying animals in the Asian and African skies. They live in the mountains, where the wind is sure to blow. Because they cannot flap their giant wings hard enough to get airborne, they need the frequent gusts of air rising off cliffs to lift them into the sky.

Once airborne, though, there's no stopping them. Airplane pilots have seen griffon vultures flying at over 30,000 feet (9,144 m), where the air is very cold. How they keep their eyeballs from freezing is a mystery. Perhaps that's why these birds are named after a mythical animal—a fantastic gryphon, a beast with the body of a lion and the wings and head of an eagle. From their perch in the stratosphere, they can see vast distances, searching for dead cattle, yaks, sheep, and sometimes humans.

STORKS— A DISTANT RELATIVE

In old fairy tales, vultures bring death and storks bring life, carrying babies in their beaks. It seems as though these fairy tales knew what scientists only recently learned. Storks and New World vultures shared a common ancestor millions of years ago.

Storks are large, long-legged waterbirds that have big beaks and wide wings designed for soaring. They are also some of the tallest birds in the world. The largest kinds of storks are bareheaded so mud and blood does not soil their feathers. Some feed on carrion, others on fish, frogs, mice, and insects in open fields, shallow water, or wet, grassy areas.

These birds often nest with other waterbirds in dense colonies in trees. However, the European white

Vultures and storks often feed side by side.

stork nests on chimneys and telephone poles and probably inspired the myth that storks bring babies.

The most common stork in the southern United States is the wood stork. These storks feed in groups and probe the mud with their large beaks that curve downward, feeling the muddy water for fleeing fish. Graceful fliers, wood storks soar for hours on end, often in the company of vultures. With their white wings and black wingtips, they resemble the king vultures in flight. Like vultures, they cannot vocalize.

Some bareheaded storks in Europe, Africa, and Asia look and act like vultures. In Africa, the marabou stork stands over 5 feet (1.5 m) tall. With its enormous daggerlike beak, it often steals bits of food from vultures. This bird also eats flamingoes, stabbing them when it raids waterbird colonies. In India, the 4-foot- (1.2-m-) tall adjutant stork circles on thermals with vultures and then fights with them over the same carcasses. In the language of India, they are known as bone swallowers. Adjutant storks are now very rare.

Imagine a vulture as big as a Cadillac and you have an idea what a teratorn was like. With a 22-foot (6.7-m) wingspread and a monstrous beak, this extinct bird is related to storks and vultures. Bones of the smaller teratornis, with 12-foot (3.7-m) wings, are found in the tar pits of Rancho La Brea in Los Angeles.

In the Pleistocene Ice Age, pools of oil seeped to the surface of the earth and attracted animals that thought these tar pits were water holes. Teratornis and California condors also got tarry feathers when eating dead animals trapped in the tar. Unlike bloody gore, the tar would not wash off, and the birds died in the pools of oil, which preserved their bones.

Surprisingly, the remains of Old World vultures have also been found at the New World tar pits. It would not have been difficult for such large birds to fly across the land bridges that connected the Old and New Worlds thousands of years ago when the ocean levels were lower. It is strange, however, that these birds died out so relatively recently (vultures are, after all, millions of years old), once again leaving the Old and New World vultures isolated on their own continents of origin.

People have always found vultures intriguing.

PEOPLE AND VULTURES

No wonder we are fascinated by vultures. With their wings outstretched, they are bigger than people!

There is a long history of human fascination with vultures. Four thousand years ago, the ancient Egyptians considered the griffon vulture to be a form of the goddess named Nekhbet. King Tut was buried with a necklace of the vulture goddess lying on his chest for protection. And the kings' wives wore gold-wire head-dresses in the shape of Nekhbet, holding in her claws the symbol of infinity. It's easy to understand why, if you've ever seen a griffon vulture fly off with only a few flaps of the wings, circle upward, and disappear out of sight. It looks as though it flew to the sun or forever into infinity.

Fascination with vultures dates back to ancient times.

Throughout history, vultures' recycling of energy by eating the dead has inspired humans to appreciate the cycle of nature. To the Mayans of Mexico, king vultures were the symbol of rain, which signaled the return of life. Three thousand years ago, king vultures appeared in stone carvings as godlike figures. Even today, Tibetan Buddhists set their dead relatives on "celestial burial platforms" where vultures recycle human remains. A religious group in India also built special "towers of silence" where red-headed and white-backed vultures can consume the deceased.

On the other side of the world, Native Americans sought to honor the California condor, which they called Thunderbird, by drawing and painting its likeness on stone and sand. They even wove the vulture's image into reed baskets and wool blankets.

However, cowboys and gold miners felt differently. Some cowboys used to shoot the large birds right out of the sky. They also poisoned coyotes and wolves, which inadvertently killed any condors that fed on the poisoned carcasses. Then museum collectors took their share of condor specimens and eggs. Even the miners who rushed to California for gold in 1849 used condor quills to store gold dust.

Condors began to die faster than they were reproducing. By 1890, there were less than two hundred. The flock continued to dwindle, and by 1953, there were sixty. By 1980, only about twenty-one condors were left in the wild. The condors seemed doomed to join teratornis and mammoths in extinction.

In 1987, scientists captured the last wild condor to protect it. The bird was added to a captive flock of condors in the San Diego and Los Angeles zoos. Surprisingly, the captive birds bred better than anyone thought they would. By 1994, the zoo flock grew from an all-time low of twenty-seven to eighty-eight.

On January 14, 1992, an historic event took place: condors were returned to the wilds of the Los Padres National Forest in California. However, soon after release, some birds died after hitting powerlines, eating dead animals shot with poisonous lead bullets, and drinking antifreeze spilled from a car. Without adult condors to guide them, the naturally curious young condors did not fare well in a world full of human dangers.

The remaining condors were quickly returned to the zoos. This time, the zookeepers kept the birds isolated to prevent them from associating people with food and trained the birds to avoid humans. In August

The California condor, shown here in captivity, is one of the most endangered birds in the world.

The threatened Eurasian black vulture is one of the biggest and heaviest birds of flight.

1995, condors were released and a flock of thirteen survive. Future releases will take place in the Grand Canyon of Arizona and southern New Mexico. So far this program has cost over 20 million dollars.

In south central France, where humans had decimated the griffon vulture population, a program was begun to reintroduce the birds to the region. It was designed to take advantage of the highly social behavior of griffon vultures, which nest in groups on cliffs. Birds raised in zoos were held in the nesting area and released just as breeding season began. Instead of getting lost in the mountains, they remained in the area to breed.

Other conservation projects to reestablish the bearded vulture in the European Alps and to release the Eurasian black vulture into the mountains of France are in the works. As the California condor project shows, however, bringing back vultures once they have almost entirely died out is extremely expensive.

In other parts of the world, vultures are still in danger. Poisons used to control rodents kill vultures in China and feather collectors threaten vulture populations in the former Soviet Union. Others, who believe vultures help spread disease, kill thousands of the birds each year. But the vultures' role in the environment is crucial, as the people of Hinckley, Ohio, seem to know.

As the world's best recyclers, vultures have much to teach us.

Hinckley hosts a festival celebrating the annual return of vultures. Turkey vultures have been coming here in flocks since the Great Hinckley Hunt of 1818, when local farmers hunted and killed many animals that were destroying their crops. Piles of carcasses attracted swarms of vultures and today their ancestors keep coming back. Since 1957, Buzzard Sunday has taken place on the Sunday following March 15 at Hinckley Reservation, a nature preserve south of Cleveland, Ohio.

Perhaps we should take a tip from the folks in Hinckley and leave the vultures alone. By cleaning up after humans, vultures have learned the skills of recycling and sanitation. If we could learn to be such good energy savers and recyclers, the world would be a cleaner and better place.

A NOTE FROM THE AUTHOR

Many vultures species, including the California condor and griffon vulture, are endangered. To learn about ways to help vultures, hawks, and eagles, contact HawkWatch International at the following address.

HawkWatch International
P.O. Box 660
Salt Lake City, UT 94110

FOR FURTHER READING

Arnold, Caroline. *On the Brink of Extinction: The California Condor.* New York: Harcourt Brace, 1993.

Boyer, Trevor, ed. *Eagles.* San Diego: Wildlife Education, 1985.

Burnie, David. *Bird.* New York: Knopf Books for Young Readers, 1988.

Burton, Maurice. *Birds.* New York: Facts on File, 1985.

Harris, Alan, ed. *Birds.* New York: Dorling Kindersley, 1993.

Olsen, Penny. *Falcons and Hawks.* New York: Facts on File, 1992.

Peters, Westberg. *Condor.* New York: Crestwood House, 1990.

Witmer, Lawrence M. *The Search for the Origin of Birds.* New York: Franklin Watts, 1995.

INDEX

Italicized page numbers refer to illustrations.

ABOUT
THE AUTHOR

Mark J. Rauzon is an environmental consultant and a writer-photographer who travels widely. He has worked as a biologist for the U.S. Fish and Wildlife Service and served as chair of the Pacific Seabird Group. Mr. Rauzon is the author of several children's books about animals, including *Parrots*, *Seabirds*, and *Hummingbirds* for Franklin Watts. He lives in Oakland, California.